CSS

For Beginners

The Best CSS Guide For Beginners To Learn Learn CSS in One Day and Developing a Strong Coding Foundation

By

Ethan Hall

introduction **TO CSS** FOR BEGINNERS

ICANBUILDABLOG.COM

trademarks and brands within this book are for clarifying purposes only and are owned by the owner, not affiliated with this document.

Contents

Introduction

CSS was introduced by Hakom Lie in 1996 and collaborate by Bert Bos. Designed to be used in conjunction with HTML. CSS is used to style a web browser or HTML code. CSS specifies how HTML components should be rendered. Cascading Style Sheets is the programming language used to style web material.

Using CSS, we may adjust the presentation and style of the webpage. We may also specify how a website's appearance varies on various platforms, such as handheld devices, personal computers, and tablets. CSS is not a scripting language in the same way as JavaScript or C++ are. CSS, on the other hand, is also not as simple as it appears. You may have problems with web creation if you want to do it without learning. As a result, studying CSS is almost as useful as we learn a programming language. CSS greatly improves the graphic appearance of a website.

Chapter-1: What is CSS?

CSS is an abbreviation of Cascading Style Sheets. The focus is on "Style." It is just a style sheet language. It is not a mark-up language that is used to describe the appearance of a written text, such as HTML and is in charge of how the web pages will appear. CSS specifies how HTML items can appear on paper, screen, and in all other mediums. CSS is simple to learn and comprehend. CSS is most widely seen in conjunction with the scripting languages such as HTML as well as XHTML.

The fact that CSS cascades are a pretty cool function. Cascading implies that using certain guidelines, one or many style sheets may be added to an HTML document consecutively. This priority-cascading scheme is consistent. CSS helps you save time and effort. It has the ability to monitor the structure of several web pages at the same time. As a result, the same tag will have several types. For fifty pages of a website, a Web developer might choose to reduce the standard text size around 16pt to 12pt. If all of the pages have same style sheet, changing the text size on the style sheet would cause all of the pages to display the tiny text.

In brief, you could use it for styling HTML documents like page fonts, table sizes, layouts, and colors. Cascading Style Sheets CSS files store external stylesheets.

You can also make the most current design take precedence over previous styles. For instance, with CSS, we may specify that each of the text should be 14px high. We may even claim later that we like it to be blue in color. Later, we can make one sentence bold or that green should be used instead of blue color.

Although CSS is well known for designing text styles, but it can also be used to format other elements of a Web page's architecture. CSS may be used to describe picture padding, the thickness, design, and color of a border of the table and the padding of table cells and other items. CSS allows Web designers more precise command over the appearance of Web pages than HTML does. This is the reason that most modern Web sites use CSS.

You may also use the CSS language to apply effects or graphics to the website. It can be used to display CSS animations such as button click effects, animated backgrounds, spinners, and loaders.

Your website will look as a simple HTML page if you don't use CSS. If we disable Facebook's CSS, this is what it would look like:

Jump to
Sections of this page
Accessibility help
Press alt + / to open this menu

Facebook

Email or Phone   Password
                                            Log In
                        Forgotten account?
Facebook helps you connect and share with the people in your life.

Create an account
It's quick and easy.
An error occurred. Please try again.
We couldn't create your account
We were not able to sign you up for Facebook.
First name
Surname
Mobile number or email addr
Re-enter email address
New password
Birthday
14 ▼ Jan ▼ 1995 ▼
Gender
Female Male Custom
Select your pronoun   ▼
Your pronoun is visible to everyone.
Gender (optional)

By clicking Sign Up, you agree to our Terms, Data Policy and Cookie Policy. You may receive SMS notifications from us and can opt out at any time.

1.1 CSS Versions

CSS1 (Level 1) was released as a suggestion by the World Wide Web Consortium (W3C) during 1996 in the month of December. This edition includes a basic visual styling model across every HTML tag, as well as a summary of the CSS language.

CSS2 is recommended by W3C that is constructed on CSS1 (Cascading Style Sheets, level 1) and was released in May 1998. Style sheets that are Media-specific, such as printers as well as element placement, downloadable fonts and tables, have been included in this edition.

1.2 Difference between HTML and CSS

HTML, or hypertext mark-up language, is used to create the majority of websites. This is the most popular way to add color, fonts, hyperlinks (clickable text which takes the user elsewhere), and graphic doodads. However, the size of the websites can increase. When this occurs, HTML becomes very difficult to perform a very simple task. Cascading style sheets can create web site's design simple once more!

Consider CSS to be a dress code for computers. CSS is mostly used to illustrate how web pages can appear. Much better, Cascading style sheets can be conveniently removed from HTML, making it easier to locate the dress code. It updates the appearance of your website quickly and can edit it easily. You should adjust your CSS, much as a uniform at school, and your student's appearance can change as well. Style sheets encourage you to quickly update whole websites if you want, similar to how a fashionista encourages people to evolve with time whilst also being the same individuals. CSS can make the website more colorful, nicer, and clearer, while HTML merely creates the foundation or the skeleton.

1.3 Difference between HTML and CSS

It is briefly explained here:

S.NO.	HTML	CSS
1.	HTML stands for **H**yper **T**ext **M**arkup **L**anguage.	CSS stands for **C**ascading **S**tyle **S**heets.
2.	It is a basic mark-up language.	It is an extension of HTML
3.	It is used to describe the layout of a web page.	It is used to style web pages by utilizing various styling features.
4.	HTML consists of tags in which text is enclosed.	CSS consists of declaration and selectors blocks.
5.	Visualization and presentation can not be done by HTML.	Visualization and presentation can be done by CSS.
6.	It has less support and backup.	It has higher support and backup.
7.	HTML can not be used inside a CSS sheet.	CSS can be used inside an HTML document.
8.	HTML doesn't have any types.	CSS has two types: internal or external which depending on the requirement.

Html Example

```html
<html>
<body>
        <h1>This is an HTML example</h1>
</body>
</html>
```

Output:

This is a HTML example

CSS Example

```html
<html>
<head>
<style>
body {
background-color:orange;
}
</style>
</head>
<body>

<h1>This is a CSS example</h1>

<p>This page has orange background color</p>

</body>
```

```
</html>
```

Output:

This is a CSS example

This page has orange background color

1.4 Advantages of CSS

Following are the advantages of the CSS:

- CSS saves you time by allowing you to write CSS once and reuse it through several pages.
- Cascading sheets simplify website creation and management by affecting the entire website with a single line of code update.
- CSS provides a wider variety of features and better styles than HTML.
- Since there is fewer coding on the page, it takes less time for it to load.
- Compatibility for a variety of devices.
- Uses an offline cache to allow for offline surfing.
- The script ensures platform independence as well as it is compatible with the most recent browsers.
- HTML attributes still are frowned upon, and it is recommended that all HTML sites use Cascading Style Sheet to ensure compatibility with potential browsers.
- The user can easily modify the online web page.

- Since it is less complicated, the work required is greatly decreased.
- It decreases the size of a transferring file.
- To improve site speed, web designers can use a few lines of code for each website.

1.5 Disadvantages of CSS

Following are the disadvantages of the CSS:

- When it comes to CSS, what fit's in one browser may not fit in another. The web developers could verify the program's consistency by running it in different browsers.
- If any incompatibilities arise after making the modifications, we must check the consistency. All browsers are affected by the same change.
- CSS, especially CSS 1 to CSS 3, causes web browsers to become confused.
- Different browsers handle CSS in different ways. CSS is supported differently in Internet Explorer and Opera.

1.6 Importance of CSS

Web pages were severely limited in function and appearance prior to the W3C development of CSS in 1996. A website was shown as plain images, text, hypertext, and links to many other hyperlinks sites in early browsers. There was no style at all, just a simple column of paragraphs running around the paper.

CSS enabled web designers to do things like:

- specify new fonts besides the browser's default fonts
- specify colors and size of links and text
- add colors to the backgrounds

- include webpage elements into boxes and move certain boxes to unique locations on the website

They added "style" to style sheets, allowing for the very first time the design of Web pages.

W3C was the initial commercial browser that interprets and use CSS in 1998. Support for such CSS functions varies from website to website to this day. The W3C, which continues to oversee and develop Web standards, just published a new CSS and CSS3 standard. Developers of CSS3 expect that all web browsers can interpret and view all CSS functions in the same manner.

1.7 WHY should everyone learn CSS?

There is a number of websites who offer free or low-cost templates, but even that restricts how much we can develop and leaves us with a site that resembles just like everyone else's. The most popular websites are those that stick out, are entertaining, and unforgettable in their representation of your brand. We want to attract the consumers to make an order, recommend a friend to our services, or become regular customers. We risk getting overlooked if our page mixes with the audience.

Knowing how to create our website with Hypertext Markup Language, CSS allows us to look unique from the audience with a genuine, hand-crafted illustration of our company or any major company. Saving money on any potential websites we may like to build and create good websites with CSS and HTML.

1.8 How can CSS help you?

Cascading Style Sheets can help you in many ways. Some of them are mentioned below:

i.   **Important for web designers**

CSS is a useful method of controlling the appearance of web pages. Text, fonts, colors, borders, design and backgrounds are all controlled by CSS. CSS has a number of major benefits over other web design methods.

ii. Redesign Website Quickly

It's challenging to redesign several older websites which were designed without CSS. However, if a site is created with CSS, it can easily be revamped. Backgrounds and colors can change the appearance of a website with little effort. Now, many sites make special editions of their websites for special events, and they may take less time to create an alternative style sheet.

iii. Change Website Designs

It's simple to create a website using a free Web design. However, these designs are rarely elegant, so your website would resemble any other online website. You may change these designs using CSS to show your styles and colors. As a result, you'll get a personalized website without putting in a lot of work.

iv. To Earn Money

You can offer these facilities to other websites once you've mastered CSS. And if you want to work as a freelance or independent web designer, you won't succeed much unless you know CSS.

v. To Save Money

There are several web designers that can create your CSS or website for you. However, even though you just pay them to create the designs and you manage the content, hiring someone else may be costly. When you encounter minor bugs that you can solve yourself, understanding how to update the CSS can save you money. You'll be capable of solving larger and more challenging issues when you practice.

vi.   Build Diverse Websites

CSS allows pages to appear very distinct from one website to the next without requiring a lot of code. Some websites, for example, now use subtle color differences across various parts of the web pages. You may use page IDs to modify the Cascading Style Sheet for each segment while keeping the same HTML layout. The content and CSS are the only things that alter.

1.9 Is CSS worth it?

HTML and CSS are definitely worth learning. CSS is an interesting language because, although it's fundamentals are easy, it is immensely complex and allows you full access to the world's most efficient rendering engine: the browser.

You can use the rendering engine to generate documents and apps on every device on earth. Browsers and the internet are not only the greatest way to deliver software to billions of people around the globe, but they also provide you access to the native innovation world.

Native mobile apps have browsers such as CSS, HTML, and JavaScript, which is the most famous development framework for native mobile apps. Electron, which allows you to package CSS, HTML, and JavaScript for the desktop, is used to create desktop applications like Skype, Slack, Atom, and many more. CSS gives you access to the whole world.

Chapter-2: Basic of CSS

Let's learn some basics of the Cascading Style Sheets.

2.1 How does CSS work?

To grasp the fundamentals of CSS, you should first grasp a clear understanding of modern HTML. The "box model" is used by web designers to set out web pages. A Web page is made up of a collection of boxes, each of which contains a distinct feature. The boxes are clustered, meaning they are one within the other.

A page's header, for example, is just a box that includes many smaller boxes that include many of the elements that make a header, such as a logo, navigation, shopping cart buttons, and so on. A developer adds different styles to a "header" box using CSS. Let's imagine that the developer renders the text within the header purple, which has Arial font and is fifteen points bigger in this case.

The "cascading" aspect of CSS falls into action here. The font types used in the header are applied across all of the items inside the header. Elements like navigation, links, and calls to action would all be in purple color, Arial, and fifteen points bigger.

2.2 Implementation of CSS code in HTML

You may also be thinking that how this Cascading Style Sheet coding is implemented to HTML text. CSS is written in plain text using a word processor or text editor on your device, similar to HTML. There are three ways to use CSS in HTML documents:

- Inline CSS
- Internal CSS

- External CSS

Note: In external Cascading Style Sheets, we have the styles, which is a very popular way to implement CSS. But you may also use Inline CSS and Internal CSS depending on your needs.

2.2.1 Inline CSS

An inline Cascading Style Sheets is used to give a distinctive style to a particular HTML element, which is located in the body section. The style attribute is used to specify this type of style inside an HTML tag. You won't need to use selectors for that kind of CSS design because you'll just need to apply a style attribute into every HTML tag. As a result, Inline CSS appears right next to the component it picks.

This CSS form is not suggested since every HTML tag must be styled separately. Only if you are using inline CSS, handling your website can become too difficult. Inline Cascading Style Sheets in HTML, on the other hand, maybe helpful in certain cases. For instance, if you can't access the CSS files and you just need to add styles to a particular element.

Example

Consider the following example. We apply inline CSS to <p> and <h1> tags here:

```
<!DOCTYPE html>
<html>
<body style="background-color:black;">
<h1 style="color:white;padding:30px;">Applying inline CSS</h1>
<p style="color:white;">This is an Inline example.</p>
</body>
</html>
```

Output:

Example 2

```
<!DOCTYPE html>
<html>
<body style="background-color:black;">
<h1  style="font-size:40px;color:violet;">Watch this headline</h1>
<p style="color:white;">This is an Inline example.</p>
</body>
</html>
```

Output:

Example Explained

<h1 style="font-size:40px;color:violet;">Watch this headline</h1>
Above line of code would cause one specific headline on a single .html page to appear in violet, 40 point font.

Benefits of Inline CSS

Benefits of the inline CSS are as under:

- Adding Cascading Style Sheets rules to the HTML page is simple and convenient. As a result, this method is suitable for previewing or testing the modifications to the website as well as making fast fixes.
- As opposed to the external format, you do not need to develop and upload documents separately.

Drawbacks of Inline CSS

Drawbacks of the inline CSS are as under:

- Adding Cascading Style Sheets rules to each HTML element takes time and leaves the HTML layout unorganized.

- Styling various elements will influence the size and duration of downloading your website.

2.2.2 Internal CSS

Internal CSS is also defined as Embedded Cascading Style Sheets because it's used to add a style to a single HTML page.

Internal CSS is specified in the <head> portion of a Hyper Text Markup Language (HTML) page, inside <style>...</style> i.e., the CSS is located inside an HTML file.

Internal Cascading Style Sheets are typically used when the entire page has a single specific design for each component. Moreover, using this design for different sites takes time since CSS rules must be added to each page on the website.

Example

```
<!DOCTYPE html>
<html>
<head>
<style>
body {background-color: powderblue;}
h1   {color: blue;}
p    {color: red;}
</style>
</head>
<body>

<h1>This is a heading in blue color</h1>
<p>This is a paragraph in red color.</p>
```

```
</body>
</html>
```

Output:

This is a heading in blue color

This is a paragraph in red color.

Benefits of Internal CSS

Benefits of the internal CSS are as under:

- Using the same style on different sites takes time, so CSS rules must be added to each page on the website.
- In this style sheet, you can apply ID and class selectors.

Example

```
.class {
    property1 : value1;
    property2 : value2;
    property3 : value3;
}

#id {
    property1 : value1;
    property2 : value2;
    property3 : value3;
}
```

Drawbacks of Internal CSS

The drawback of the internal CSS is:

- Applying the code into an HTML document will make the page size larger and take longer to load.

2.2.3 External CSS

For certain HTML pages, an external CSS is applied to describe the style. External CSS is a separate CSS file that only contains style property through tag attributes (for example, class, id, heading, and so on). CSS properties can be written in a different file with the .css extension that can be generated using a text editor of any type on your monitor (for example, Notepad++) and can be added to the HyperText Markup Language (HTML) document by using the link tag. This CSS approach is more effective, especially when styling a huge website. You can modify the whole site by modifying a single.css file.

By using an external CSS, you must have the header section in the .html files that connects to external CSS which appears like this:

```
<head>
<link rel="stylesheet" type="text/css" href=mysitestyle.css">
</head>
```

This would connect a .html file with the external CSS, and all the CSS commands within the file will be applied to the .html pages connected to it.

Example

Attach a link to an external CSS in to the <head> portion of every HTML page to use it:

```
<!DOCTYPE html>
<html>
<head>
```

```
    <link rel="stylesheet" href="styles.css">
</head>
<body>


<h1>This is a heading in blue color</h1>
<p>This is a paragraph in red color.</p>


</body>
</html>
```

Output:

This is a heading in blue color

This is a paragraph in red color.

Any text editor can be used to create the external CSS. The file should be saved with the .css extension and should not have any HTML code.

Here is how the "styles.css" file will look like:

"styles.css":

```
body {
  background-color: powderblue;
}
h1 {
color: blue;
}
```

```
p {
 color: red;
}
```

Benefits of External CSS

The benefits of the external CSS are as under:

- The HTML files would have a clearer layout because the CSS coding is located in a different document.
- The coding is easy to manage.
- It decreases the amount of code in half.
- Rather than making adjustments to several HTML files, we may make changes to only one file.
- Multiple pages make use of the same .css doc/files.

Drawbacks of External CSS

Drawbacks of the external CSS are as under:

- Once the external style sheet is loaded, the pages can not work correctly.
- Linking or uploading to several CSS files will extend the time it takes for your site to load.

To use External CSS

For using external CSS, follow these steps:

1. Using the text editor, make a new .css document and apply the style rules.

2. After the <title> tag, in <head> portion of a HTML sheet, add a link to the external .css file.

Remember to replace style.css and name it as your own .css file.

External CSS is a most effective way to implement Cascading Style Sheets on the website (it's easy to be aware of and create a website's style from the specific CSS file), whereas inline style and internal CSS could be used on a particular instance where individual style improvements are required.

2.3 Syntax

CSS syntax is made up of a series of rules. CSS syntax is divided into three sections:

- Selectors
- Declaration
- Property

2.3.1 Selectors

This is the name of the HTML component at the beginning of the ruleset. It specifies the styled element(s). To put it another way, a Selector will be any tag to which you choose to apply styles. Modify the selector to style a new element. Selectors include h1 to h6, id, p, class, and others.

2.3.2 Declaration

The CSS language's core feature is to set CSS properties to unique values. A declaration is a value and property pair, and every CSS engine determines which declarations refer to each and every element on a page in order to properly layout and style it.

A colon separates the name and value of the CSS property that includes in each declaration. For Example:

It is one rule, like color: blue;. It defines which property of an element you would like to style. Declaration block is enclosed by curly braces and includes one or multiple declarations divided by semicolons.

One or multiple property-value pairs make up the declaration block.

2.3.3 Property

The property is an identifier that can be a name that specifies which attribute is taken into account.

The HTML element may be styled in a variety of ways. In Cascading Style Sheets, you can choose the properties you want the rule to affect.

Property value

Property value is declared just after the colon on the right side of the property. This selects out of the several potential appearances for a specific needed property from a large number of options. A collection of valid values exists for each property. CSS is case-insensitive by nature with all properties and values.

Example

All <p> components in this example will be center-aligned and have a red text color:

```
p {
  color: red;
  text-align: center;
}
```

Output:

Hello World!

These paragraphs are styled with CSS.

Example Explained

- p is a CSS selector (it refers to the HTML attribute <p> that you need to style).
- In this property is color, and property value is red.

- Same in this case, the property is text-align, and the property value is center.

CSS Syntax

CSS has several syntaxes, such as the standard syntax, which is straightforward but does not provide much help.

You have to be familiar with the following syntax:

- Color syntax
- Margin Syntax
- White space syntax
- The syntax for CSS pseudo-classes
- Pseudo-element syntax
- Attribute selector syntax
- Background-color syntax
- Borders syntax
- Padding syntax
- Height and width syntax
- Fonts syntax
- The syntax for links, tables, lists.

2.4 Ruleset

A ruleset is a name given to the whole framework. In layman's terms, it's a series of laws. A law, also known as a "ruleset," is a declaration that instructs browsers on how to display certain elements over an HTML page. One or more comma separates every declaration block that are conditions that select certain elements of the web page. A ruleset, or rule, is made up of a selector group and a related declarations block. In the illustration below, a Cascading Style Sheets rule is depicted:

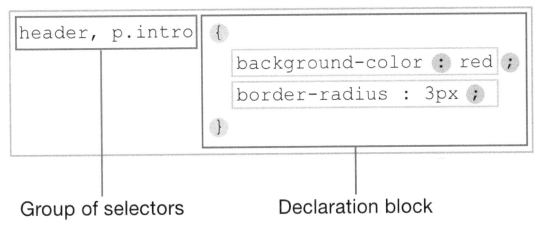

Group of selectors   Declaration block

Take note of the other main elements of the syntax:

- Each ruleset, with the exception of the selector, must be enclosed in curly braces. ({})
- Use a colon (:) to distinguish the property with it's values inside each declaration.
- Each declaration must be separated from each other by a semicolon (;) inside each ruleset.

Example

To change several property values inside a single ruleset, use semicolons to divide them, as in:

```
p {
  color: red;
  width: 500px;
  border: 1px solid black;
}
```

Breaking it down:

- Everything here is a set of rules (ruleset).
- Everything within these curly braces is the declaration block.
- A selector is a little part before the starting curly brace.

- A declaration is a key or value pair divided by the colon and terminating in a semicolon.
- Property (property name) is a key, and value (property value) is a value in these value keys or pairs.

2.5 Selectors Types

Let's discuss some types of selectors.

2.5.1 Simple selectors

CSS has a few basic selectors for selecting elements:

- Element Selector
- id Selector
- Class Selector

Element Selector

It uses the element name to pick HTML elements. Type selector or a tag is another name for it.

Example

On this page, all <p> elements have a blue text color and have center-alignment:

```
p {
  text-align: center;
  color: blue;
}
```

Output:

Every paragraph will be affected by the style.

Me too!

And me!

id Selector

The id attribute is used to select an element that is based on it's (id attribute's) value. Since the element's id is unique inside a page, the id selector can often use to pick only one specific element. Write # (hash) character preceded by the element's id to pick an element having a unique id.

Syntax

#idname

Example

The following CSS rule will be added to an HTML element having the id="para1" attribute.

```
#para1 {
  text-align: center;
  color: Green;
}
```

Output:

Hello World!

This paragraph is not affected by the style.

Note: A number cannot be the first character in the ID name.

Class Selector

The class selector is used to selecting the HTML elements that have a certain class attribute.

Type a period (.), accompanied by the name of a class so that we can select elements that have a particular class.

Syntax

.classname

Example

Every HTML element that have class="center" will be center-aligned and red in this case:

```
.center {
 text-align: center;
  color: red;
}
```

Output:

Red and center-aligned heading

Red and center-aligned paragraph.

Note: You might even decide that a class can have an impact on a particular HTML element.

Example 2

In the following example, only the <p> elements having the class="center" would be center-aligned and red.

```
p.center {
 text-align: center;
  color: red;
}
```

Output:

This heading will not be affected

This paragraph will be red and center-aligned.

Note: HTML elements may also be used to apply to several classes.

2.5.2 More Selectors

A few more selectors are as follow:

- Combinator selectors
- Pseudo-elements selectors
- Pseudo-class selectors
- Attribute selectors

Combinator selectors

It selects elements that are based on their unique relationship, while selectors in Cascading Style Sheets are used to style the content. A Cascading Style Sheets selector could be either basic or complicated, consisting of several selectors linked together by combinators. We may, for example, target just child elements from a parent element or an element that is accompanied by another element that has the same degree.

In CSS, it has four types:

- descendant selector (space)
- child selector (>)
- adjacent sibling selector (+)
- general sibling selector (~)

Pseudo-elements selectors

It's a keyword that you may apply to a selector to style a certain part of a selected element(s). Even so, instead of adding a class to current elements, they behave as though you had applied a completely new HTML feature to the mark-up. A double colon precedes pseudo-elements (::).

Syntax

It's syntax is:

```
selector::pseudo-element {
  property: value;
}
```

It may, for example, be used to:

- Style an element's first word or line.
- Add content before or after an element's content.

Example

::first-line, for example, is used to modify the font of a paragraph's first line.

```
p::first-line {
  color: blue;
  text-transform: uppercase;
}
```

Note: In the beginning, only one colon was used for pseudo-elements, so you could see it sometimes in earlier examples or codes. For the backward compatibility, modern browsers use the old pseudo-elements of single or double colon syntax.

Pseudo-class selectors

It's a keyword that is applied to the selector to pick elements that are based on a specific state. They behave as though you had added a class to a section of a document, resulting in more versatile, manageable code and, in many cases, reducing the number of classes in a mark-up. There are numerous other pseudo-classes to choose from. Keywords that begin with a colon are known as pseudo-classes.

For Example, it's uses are:

- It is used to style differently to the visited and unvisited links
- It style's an element when it is hovered over by a mouse pointer

- It style's an element when it is focused

Syntax

It's syntax is:

selector:pseudo-class {

  property: value;

}

For example, when the user's cursor hovers over a button, :hover can change it's color.

button:hover {

  color: blue;

}

Attribute selectors

It is used to choose an element that has a particular attribute value or attribute. The Attribute selector pairs items depending on whether or not they have a specific attribute. Attribute selectors are a simple and efficient way to add styles to HTML elements depending on the existence of a certain attribute value or attribute. By default, they are case-sensitive and enclosed in brackets [].

All of the <a> elements that have target attribute are selected in the following example:

Example

a[target] {

 background-color: yellow;

}

Output:

CSS [attribute] Selector

The links with a target attribute gets a yellow background:

w3schools.com disney.com wikipedia.org

Chapter 3: CSS Box Model

It's only normal to want more power over the functionality and design of your WordPress site while you run it yourself. CSS is one of the most useful ways for changing the appearance of a website. With CSS knowledge, you can alter anything from the layout of the page to the colors, fonts, and background images.

The CSS box model is among the most fundamental principles to learn all of this. It's a basic web design principle. Understanding it allows you to quite endlessly modify the style of your website to your liking.

To use CSS effectively, you must first know that everything on a website page is comprised of rectangles. Rectangular boxes are stacked parallel on top of, to, underneath, and enclosed inside each other on every website you visit.

3.1 What exactly is a box model?

When discussing about layout and design in CSS, the expression "box model" is often used. The CSS box model is a box which wraps around any HTML element that has content, height and width. We can use it as a set of tools for personalizing the design of various elements or aligning them with one another. This involves adjusting the size, color, and position of the settings. The box model helps one to create space between elements and adds a border around them. This box is made up of several levels, so you can control it separately using CSS. This enables you to organize elements in various ways in comparison to each other and apply styles to them in a variety of ways.

Example

The box model is shown as follows:

```css
div {
  width: 300px;
  border: 15px
solid green;
padding: 50px;
 margin: 20px;
}
```

Output:

Demonstrating the Box Model

The CSS box model is essentially a box that wraps around every HTML element. It consists of: borders, padding, margins, and the actual content.

This text is the content of the box. We have added a 50px padding, 20px margin and a 15px green border. Ut enim ad minim veniam, quis nostrud exercitation ullamco laboris nisi ut aliquip ex ea commodo consequat. Duis aute irure dolor in reprehenderit in voluptate velit esse cillum dolore eu fugiat nulla pariatur. Excepteur sint occaecat cupidatat non proident, sunt in culpa qui officia deserunt mollit anim id est laborum.

3.2 Box Model Properties

It's properties are:

- Content Area
- Width
- Height
- Padding
- Borders
- Margins

Note: The other properties, with the exception of width and height, are optional. That means we can also have a box without a border, padding, or margin.

The below diagram makes it easier for you to understand:

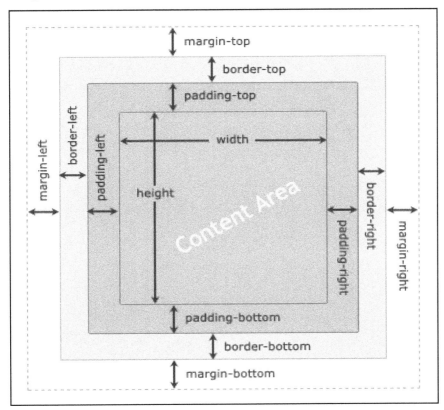

3.2.1 Content Area

This section contains content such as images, text, and other media. The content edge defines it's boundaries, and the height and width of the content box determine it's dimensions. It has some properties added to it.

3.2.2 Width

It is the width of an element's content area. This is set to 100% by default for the block elements. Inline elements may take up as much room as their content requires. It can have a value of auto, percentage, or length. When you use CSS to set the width of the element, you're really setting the width of a content area. Padding, boundaries, and margins must all be added when calculating the whole size of the element.

Example

The total width is 350px for this <div>:

```
div {
 width: 320px;
 padding: 10px;
 border: 5px
solid                                          gray;
 margin: 0;
}
```

Output:

Calculate the total width:

The picture above is 350px wide. The total width of this element is also 350px.

An element's total width must be calculated as follows:

Total width = width + left padding + right padding + left border + right border + left margin + right margin

So,

320px (width)

+ 20px (left + right padding)

+ 10px (left + right border)

+ 0px (left + right margin)

= 350px

Values

It's values are:

auto

This is the default setting. The height and width are calculated by the browser.

length

It defines height and width in pixels, centimeters, and other terms.

%

It defines the width and height of the containing block in percent.

initial

It sets height and width to their default values.

inherit

In this, the parent's height and width would be inherited.

3.2.3 Height

As you would expect, this indicates the height of an element. It is normally regulated by the data inside it, but if necessary, you may also set a certain height. Again, this is only applicable to block elements.

Example

Let's set the height and width of <div> element:

```
div {
 height: 100px;
  width: 500px;
  background-color: powderblue;
}
```

Output:

Set the height and width of an element

This div element has a height of 100px and a width of 500px.

An element's total height must be calculated as follows:

Total element height = height + top padding + bottom padding + top border + bottom border + top margin + bottom margin

So,

100px (height)

+ 20px (left + right padding)

+ 10px (left + right border)

+ 0px (left + right margin)

= 130px

Values

It's values are same as width's values.

3.2.4 Padding

This area is the space between the content area and the boundary box. Padding is a transparent layer. It's the space that surrounds a paragraph text. The width and height of a padding-box determine it's dimensions. This is essential, for example, to keep text inside of the HTML element to make it readable.

CSS padding may be changed to accomplish the following effects:

Increase the amount of space between the content and the border

It is a very popular utilization of padding, and it is very useful for adding whitespace within elements.

Alter the size of the Element

Content will have exactly the same size as before, but there will be more room around it when you rise padding value. When you try to extend the clickable region with digital elements like buttons, this is handy.

Adding some Padding

When looking at this example, the most noticeable features that we notice is the text which is directly bordering on the element's side. It causes it difficult to read and unappealing to the eyes. Fortunately, the padding clause allows us to change this. For **Example**

```
example-element {
background-color: deepskyblue;
border: 15px solid blue;
height: 300px;
padding: 16px;
width: 300px;
}
```

And the result is:

> Lorem ipsum dolor sit amet, consectetur adipiscing elit.

Keep in mind that, just as with the border, various padding values can be set on different corners/sides of the element. To do this, use padding: top;, padding: right;, padding: bottom; and padding: left;.

You may also use padding: 15px 8px 25px 5px; as a shorthand property. It shows the padding on the top, right, bottom, and left sides.

Padding is among the only few properties in this list which can be used on inline elements as well. However, be aware that the bottom and top padding can encroach on other elements, so bear that in mind.

Padding values

Lengths, percentages, and inherit are used to set padding values. It is incapable of accepting negative values. For every padding property, the original or default value is 0.

length

It specifies the padding in pt, px, cm, and other terms.

%

It specifies the padding in percent of the underlying element's width.

inherit

It specifies that padding of the child element must be inherited.

Padding of every side of the element could be defined using CSS properties:

- padding-top
- padding-right
- padding-bottom
- padding-left

Shorthand Property

It is feasible to write all padding properties inside one property to simplify the code.

It is be used for:

- padding-top
- padding-right
- padding-bottom
- padding-left

Syntax

top padding, right padding, bottom padding and left padding.

It works like this:

padding: [top] [left] [right] [bottom];

For Example

padding: 25px 50px 75px 100px;

- top padding is 25px
- right padding is 50px
- bottom padding is 75px
- left padding is 100px

Example

Shorthand property which has four values, can be shown as:

div {

 padding: 25px 50px 75px 100px;

}

Output:

The padding shorthand property - 4 values

This div element has a top padding of 25px, a right padding of 50px, a bottom padding of 75px, and a left padding of 100px.

Longhand Property

Longhand can be used to declare all padding properties individually. As a result, the above example can be re-written as:

div {

 padding-top: 25px;

 padding-right: 50px;

```
    padding-bottom: 75px;
    padding-left: 100px;
}
```

3.2.5 Margin

Finally, the term "margin" refers to the area outside the border. It is essential for page architecture, alignment, and spacing since it essentially manages the gap between various elements. Around the box, the margin is opaque. The margin-box width and height are the dimensions of the Margin area. It is beneficial to separate an element from it's neighbouring elements. Other items are moved out of the box. Margin values can be positive or negative. When you use a negative margin solely on a single side of the box, it can overlap other elements on the webpage. We may use the margin property to manage all of the element's margins at once or the corresponding longhand properties to control either side individually:

- margin-top
- margin-right
- margin-bottom
- margin-left

Basic Syntax

top-margin, right margin, a bottom margin, and left margin.

For-Example

margin: 16px 25px 30px 16px;

The top margin is 16 pixels, the right margin is 25 pixels, the bottom margin is 35 pixels, and the left margin is 16 pixels.

Margin property can define one to four values. That value is either a <length>, <percentage>, or the auto keyword.

- If only one value is defined, the same margin is applied on all four sides.
- Where two values are defined, the top and bottom margins need to apply first, followed by the left and right margins.
- Where three values are defined, the first margin is applied on top, the second on the right and left, and the third to bottom.
  - When four values are defined, the margins are applied in a clockwise direction.

Values

It's values are as follow:

length

It sets the margin's size as a constant value.

percentage

The margin's size is defined as a percentage.

auto

The browser chooses an appropriate margin to apply. This value, for example, may be used to focus an element in certain situations.

Margin Example

Set various margins on each of the <p> element's four sides:

```
p {
  margin-top: 100px;
  margin-bottom: 100px;
  margin-right: 150px;
  margin-left: 80px;
}
```

Output:

Using individual margin properties

This div element has a top margin of 100px, a right margin of 150px, a bottom margin of 100px, and a left margin of 80px.

Shorthand Syntax

margin: unit's|initial|inherit|auto;

Where unit's will use values in px, em, length, percent, and so on.

This syntax simultaneously sets values as margin-top, margin-bottom, margin-right, and margin-left.

Example

```
<style>
  .margin_shorthand1 {
    border:20px solid powderblue;
    margin: 5px;
}
  .margin_shorthand2 {
    border:15px solid orange;
    margin: 20px 10px;
}
.margin_shorthand3 {
    border:8px solid pink;
    margin: 30px 10px 20px;
```

```
}
  .margin_shorthand4 {
    border:12px solid aqua;
    margin: 0 15px 20px 5px;
}
</style>
```

Output:

If margin has 1 value

margin: 5px; means: margin-top:5px;margin-right:5px;margin-bottom:5px;margin-left:5px;

If margin has 2 values

margin: 20px 10px; means: margin-top:20px;margin-right:10px;margin-bottom:20px;margin-left:10px;

If margin has 3 values

margin: 30px 10px 20px; means: margin-top:30px;margin-right:10px;margin-bottom:20px;margin-left:10px;

If it's value is one.

For Example

margin: 10px;

then, the top, right, bottom, and the left margin is 10px each.

If it's value is two.

For Example

margin: 0.5em 1em;

then, 0.5em is set for the top and bottom margins each, while the right and left margins are 1em each.

If it's value is three.

For Example

margin: 5px 3px 8px;

then, the top margin is 5px, the right and left margins are 3px each, and the bottom margin is 8px.

If it's value is four.

For Example

margin: 10px 2em 15px 5px;

then, the top margin is 10px, the right margin is 2em, the bottom margin is 15px, and the left margin is 5px.

Margin collapsing

The idea of margin collapse is crucial to grasp when it comes to margins. If the margins of two elements touch and both are positive, the margins will merge to form a single margin, that is, the length of the biggest individual margin. When the margin is negative for one or two margins, the total will subtract the negative value.

There are two paragraphs in the below example. Top paragraph's bottom margin is 50-pixel. Top margin of the second paragraph is 30 pixels. Since margins have merged, the real margin between these boxes is 50 pixels, rather than the sum of both margins.

There are few rules that govern when margins collapse and when it does not. For the time being, the most important factor to note is that margin collapse is a real thing. This is most likely what is occurring when you use margins to create space and don't have the space you want.

3.2.6 Border

It's the straight line right outside padding and right in the middle of the margin. They come in a variety of designs, colors, and sizes. Strong, dotted, double, dashed, ridge, groove, inset, outset, or zero are all options. If desired, it can even have rounded corners. The important thing to note is that a border sit's between the padding and margin of the element, and it's usually opaque to cover some background color. The border couldn't be used to set customized value for the border-image; however, it sets itself to it's default value, which is none. The width and height of the border determine it's dimensions. The short hand border-width and border properties define the density of borders. When box-sizing property is assigned to the border-box, the height, max-height, min-height, width, max-width, and min-width properties may be used to specify the size of the border region.

Short hand border

Border property in CSS is the shorthand syntax that accepts several values to draw one line across the element. Any excluded sub-values would be set to

it's original value, like all shorthand properties.

When you need all of the boundaries to look the same, the border shorthand comes in handy. Longhand border-style, border-color and border-width properties, which acknowledge different values on each line, can be used to differentiate them. You can also use the (border-top and border-block-start) properties of the border to aim single border at one time.

Syntax

top-border, right border, bottom border, and left border.

Example

.box {

```
  border: 3px solid red;
  height: 200px;
  width: 200px;
}
```

Value

One or many of the preceding values can be used in combination with boundary property. It makes no difference what order the values are in. If the border's style isn't defined, it would be invisible. This happened because it's style is set to none by default.

It's values are:

- border-style
- border-color
- border-width

border-style

It sets the border's style. If nothing is specified, the value defaults to none.

border-color

The color of a border is set here. If no color is specified, the default color is used.

border-width

The width of a border is set here. If no value is specified, it defaults to medium.

styling borders

In CSS, there are several properties to choose from when it comes to border styling. There are only four borders, each with a different style, color and width that we can change. Border property allows you to change the style, width and color of every border in one go.

You may use the following commands to customize the properties of every side individually:

- border-top
- border-left
- border-right
- border-bottom

You may use the most detailed longhand properties to change the width, color and style of one side:

- border-top-color
- border-top-style
- border-top-width
- border-right-color
- border-right-style
- border-right-width
- border-bottom-color
- border-bottom-style
- border-bottom-width
- border-left-color
- border-left-style
- border-left-width

Using the following to set color, width and style on each side:

- border-color
- border-width
- border-style

border-color

The color of the four borders is set by this property. The value of this property can range from one to four.

The color can be adjusted using the following methods:

- **name**

    specifying it by the name of the colors, such as "blue"

- **RGB**

    Specifying it by RGB values, such as "rgb(266,0,1)"

- **HSL**

    Specifying it by HSL values, such as "hsl(0, 50%, 100%)"

- **HEX**

    Specifying it by HEX values, such as "#ff0010"

- **transparent**

Note: When border-color isn't defined, the element's color is used. Border-style property must always be set prior to the border-color property. Before you can alter the color of an element, it should have borders.

If border-color property consists of four values:

border-color: green pink blue red;

- top border is green
- right border is pink
- bottom border is blue
- left border is red

If border-color property consists of three values:

border-color: blue red green;

- top border is blue
- right and left borders are red
- bottom border is green

If border-color property consists of two values:

border-color: green red;

- top and bottom borders are green
- right and left borders are red

If border-color property consists of one value:

border-color: blue;

- all four borders are blue

Example 1

Let's add color to all borders:

```
p {
 border-style: solid;
 border-color: #ff0000                                        #0000ff;
}
```

Output:

One-colored border!

Example 2

```
p.one {
  border-style: solid;
  border-color: red              green            blue            yellow;
}
```

Output:

The border-color Property

The border-color property can have from one to four values (for the top border, right border, bottom border, and the left border):

A solid multicolor border

Border width

Border-width property determines how wide the borders of an element should be. The value of this property will range between one to four.

Examples

border-width: medium thin 10px thick;

- top border is medium
- right border is thin
- bottom border is 10px
- left border is thick

border-width: medium thick thin;
- top border is medium
- right and left borders are thick
- bottom border is thin

border-width: medium thin;
- top and bottom borders are medium
- right and left borders are thin

border-width: thick;
- all four borders are thick

Note: Border-style property should always be declared prior to border-width property. Before you set a width of an element, it must have some borders.

Example

Now let's set borders width:

div {border-width: thin;}

Output:

> # A heading with a thin border

> A div element with a thin border.

Note: The border-width property does not work if it is used alone. Use the border-style property to set the border first.

3.3 Types of Box Model

There are two types of the box model. These are as under:

3.3.1 Standard box model

When you assign a box, it's width and hight attribute in this model type, the content box's height and width are specified. The height and width of the box are then applied to random border and padding to have the overall size taken by that box. Browsers already use the same box model by default.

Example

Suppose that the box's height, width, margin, padding and border are all specified by CSS:

.box {

  width: 350px;

  height: 150px;

  margin: 10px;

```
  padding: 25px;
  border: 5px solid black;
}
```
Output:

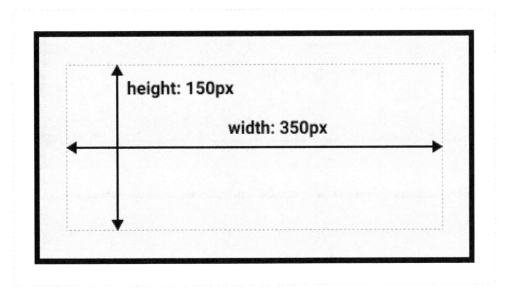

In above standard box model, the space occupied by the box would eventually be 410px (350 + 25 + 25 + 5 + 5), and it's height is 210px (150 + 25 + 25 + 5 + 5), since the border and padding was attached to the content box's width used by content box.

3.3.2 Alternative box model

You may think that adding up the padding and border to have the true size of your box is difficult, and you might be right. As a result, CSS launched an additional box model a little later than a standard box model. Every width on the webpage is the visible width of the box, so the width of the content area is the width minus the border and padding width.

Example

The following is the result of using that CSS example as before (height = 150px, width = 350px).

Output:

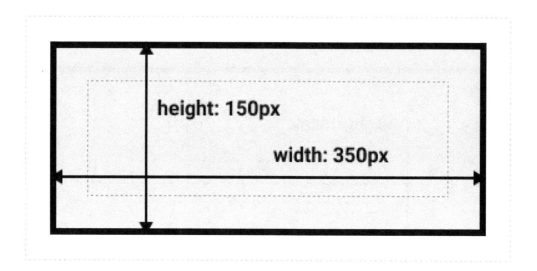

3.4 Why CSS Box Model Is Important?

You've dealt with the box model if you've ever been working on a web page layout and find yourself doing every kind of calculation to sort out how big or wide you should create things and yet have them act appropriately on the page. It's essential to comprehend how margins, borders, padding, and text all fit together to build the page's layout.

3.5 Summary of Box Model

- Boxes should be used to describe all the HTML elements present on the web page.
- The word "Box Model" in CSS defines the layout and design of a page.
- Box Model is made up of the following elements: margins, borders, padding, and the real content.

- We have the ability to modify the width and height of the elements (boxes).
- Box Model enables one to specify the amount of space between components/elements.
- We may use Box Model to insert borders across the elements.

Chapter 4: Positioning and Floating

A lack of comprehension of CSS's position, display, and float properties is among the most popular CSS issues that others are struggling with. Elements on the website will resize, rearrange and do all but what you're striving to do when you set out the designing for your website. In a frenzy of trial and error, you test any combination of various CSS properties on child and parent divs. Nothing seems to be running. You yell with frustration. There has to be a reason for the chaos. Positioning and floating make all of these easy for us.

4.1 Position

Position property defines how an object is placed on the web page or in relation to other items. Position's default value is static, which means that items displayed on the web page as same as they display on the document. The top, bottom, left, and right properties are then used to place the elements. These properties, though, position property has to be set first set in order to make these properties work. They often behave differently based on the value of the position.

It consists of five values. These are as under:

- Static
- Fixed
- Relative
- Absolute

Syntax

A single keyword, such as static, relative, fixed or absolute, is used to specify it.

Example

position: relative;

4.1.1 Types of Position

It consists of four types. These are as under:

- Static
- Fixed
- Relative
- Absolute

static

The static position is by default use for every element. The element is placed in accordance with the document's usual flow. The top, bottom, left, and right properties have little effect on static positioned components or elements.

Example

```
div.static {
  position: static;
  border: 3px solid #73AD21;
}
```

Output:

position: static;

An element with position: static; is not positioned in any special way; it is always positioned according to the normal flow of the page:

This div element has position: static;

fixed

It also excludes elements from the document's flow, just as it is done by absolute positioned components or elements. In reality, they behave almost identical; the only difference is that fixed-position components are often relative to the file or document and not with any specific parent; also, they are unchanged by scrolling. The values for right, top, left, and bottom decides it's final location.

A static element should not leave a blank space on the website where it will usually be located.

Example

```
div.fixed {
 position: fixed;
 bottom: 0;
 right: 0;
 width: 300px;
 border: 3px solid #73AD21;
}
```

Output:

position: fixed;

An element with position: fixed; is positioned relative to the viewport, which means it always stays in the same place even if the page is scrolled:

This div element has position: fixed;

relative

The element, such as static value, is placed according to the document's usual flow. However, right, left, bottom, top, and z-index can now work. The element's positional properties "push" it in that path from it's original location. Other content would not be resized to fit through the element's void.

Example

```
div.relative {
 position: relative;
 left: 30px;
 border: 3px solid #73AD21;
}
```

Output:

position: relative;

An element with position: relative; is positioned relative to its normal position:

This div element has position: relative;

absolute

When an element or a component that is completely positioned is removed from the flow, other components are placed as though they never existed. In page layout, no space is provided for the component. The position of the element with absolute position is proportional to the closest positioned ancestor.

When the absolute position element seems to have no position ancestors, it uses the document structure and scrolls with the page. Values of right, top, left, and bottom decides it's final location.

Example

```
div.relative {
position: relative;
width: 400px;
height: 200px;
border: 3px solid #73AD21;
```

```css
}

div.absolute {
 position: absolute;
 top: 80px;
right: 0;
width: 200px;
height: 100px;
border: 3px solid #73AD21;
}
```

Output:

position: absolute;

An element with position: absolute; is positioned relative to the nearest positioned ancestor (instead of positioned relative to the viewport, like fixed):

This div element has position: relative;

> This div element has position: absolute;

4.2 Floating

CSS's float property is used to position elements. We should look at the print design to grasp it's intent and origin. Images should be set on the page just like text wraps over them when required in a print design. This is referred to as "text wrap" in the industry. Here's an illustration of it.

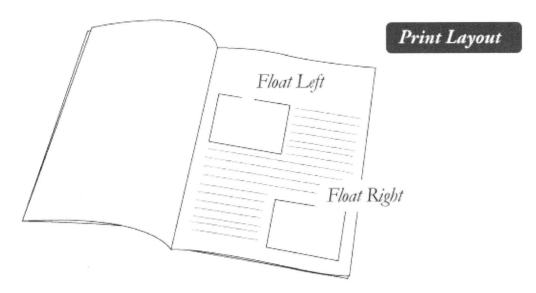

The text-holding boxes in the layout of the page's programs may be ordered to honor or ignore the text wrap. By skipping text wrap, the words would spill over the picture as though they weren't even there. That's the distinction between the image or picture being a portion of page flow or not becoming a portion of page flow. The two are very close in terms of web design.

Think about an inline variable nesting inside a <p>, such as <img>. When the float value is set to 'left,' the image will be on left side, and the text will be on the right side, wrapping to a complete line under where the image finishes. Setting the clear property on another component (as in <p> next to one floated <img>) prevents the image from floating to either or both sides. Without using tables, the float property of CSS enables a developer to use table-like columns inside the HTML layout. CSS designs will not be feasible without the CSS float attribute and would thus depend on absolute and relative positioning, which will be complicated and unmaintainable.

Note: Float property is ignored by the absolute positioned components(elements).

CSS Demo: float

float: none;

float: left;

float: right;

Syntax

- **Short-hand**

float: none|left|right|initial|inherit;

- **Long-hand**

float: left;

float: right;

float: none;

float: inherit;

float: initial;

Example

Let an image float to the right:

img {

float: right;

}

Output:

The float Property

In this example, the image will float to the right in the text, and the text in the paragraph will wrap around the image.

Lorem ipsum dolor sit amet, consectetur adipiscing elit. Phasellus imperdiet, nulla et dictum interdum, nisi lorem egestas odio, vitae scelerisque enim ligula venenatis dolor. Maecenas nisl est, ultrices nec congue eget, auctor vitae massa. Fusce luctus vestibulum augue ut aliquet. Mauris ante ligula, facilisis sed ornare eu, lobortis in odio. Praesent convallis urna a lacus interdum ut hendrerit risus congue. Nunc sagittis dictum nisi, sed ullamcorper ipsum dignissim ac. In at libero sed nunc venenatis imperdiet sed ornare turpis. Donec vitae dui eget tellus gravida venenatis. Integer fringilla congue eros non fermentum. Sed dapibus pulvinar nibh tempor porta. Cras ac leo purus. Mauris quis diam velit.

Values

There are four possible values for the float CSS property. These are as under:

- none
- left
- right
- inherit

none

It is not allowed for the element to float. For every element in the HTML page, the initial or default float value is none.

left

The element has to float to the left of the block in which it is contained.

right

The element has to float to the right of the block in which it is contained.

inherit

The float would be passed down from the parent element to the child element.

4.2.1 Clearing Floats

The CSS clear property, which allows you to "clear" floating components from the right or left side, or from both sides, of a component, is widely used to solve layout problems with floats.

Syntax

It has the following syntax:

clear: value;

Value

It's values are as under:

- left
- right
- both
- none
- inherit

left

In this value, the element has been pushed down to clear the left-floated components(elements)

Syntax

It's syntax is:

clear: left;

right

In this value, the element has been pushed down to clear the right-floated components(elements)

Syntax

It's syntax is:

clear: right;

both

The element is pushed down to clear both right and left floated components.

Syntax

It's syntax is:

clear: both;

none

To clear certain floated elements, the element would not be pushed down.

Syntax

It's syntax is:

clear: none;

inherit

The clear will be passed down from the parent element to the child element.

Syntax

It's syntax is:

clear: inherit;

Chapter 5: Display and Visibility

Now let's talk about some more CSS properties.

5.1 Display

Each website element is defined by the box that carries content and controls the number of spaces around it. We've learned how to place these boxes on the website, but there's always something we should do. The display property of CSS controls how a box displays on a page in relation to other components and also how the child elements of the box behave. To put it another way, it controls how the rectangular box of a website acts. The most strong and helpful property in CSS is the display property. This can be really helpful for designing websites that have a unique appearance but also adhering to web standards.

Syntax

display: value;

Example

Some uses of various display values are as under:

p.ex1 {display: none;}

p.ex2 {display: inline;}

p.ex3 {display: block;}

p.ex4 {display: inline-block;}

Output:

The display Property

display: none:

Lorem ipsum dolor sit amet, consectetur adipiscing elit. Etiam semper diam at erat pulvinar, at pulvinar felis blandit. Vestibulum volutpat tellus diam, consequat gravida libero rhoncus ut.

display: inline:

Lorem ipsum dolor sit amet, consectetur adipiscing elit. Etiam semper diam at erat pulvinar, at pulvinar felis blandit. HELLO WORLD! Vestibulum volutpat tellus diam, consequat gravida libero rhoncus ut.

display: block:

Lorem ipsum dolor sit amet, consectetur adipiscing elit. Etiam semper diam at erat pulvinar, at pulvinar felis blandit.

HELLO WORLD!

Vestibulum volutpat tellus diam, consequat gravida libero rhoncus ut.

Values

Some widely used display values are as under:

- block
- grid
- inline
- inline-block
- none
- flex

Brief description of these values are:

Block

This Element begins from the new line and occupies the whole width by default (if no width is specified). Other inline element or blocks can be present in it. It's purpose is to display a the element into the block element. The default block elements include <p>, <div>, <ul>, <li>, <canvas> and <h1>-<h6>.

Example

```
span {
    display: block;
}
a {
    display: block;
}
```

Output:

Visit tutorialrepublic.com

This span element generates a block box.

grid

It displays the element as the block-level of a grid container. Display property will also set the grid layout at the start.

Syntax

```
body {
  display: grid;
}
```

inline

The element will begin anywhere on a line that already exists. They are unaffected by the height and width properties. Any element with the inline display attribute became the inline element. These elements can display on a similar line as <span> elements without breaking. The default inline elements include <span>, <input>, <button> and <img>.

inline-block

This is meant to display the element as the inline-level of the block container, but the width and height can be adapted. Since grid, table, and flex are block-level components, they can be applied with them.

none

It clears the page from the desired element and all of it's children. When an entity has none value, it generates no boxes whatsoever. And if the display property's value is set to anything except none, then the child elements will not create any boxes. As a result, corresponding elements act as though this component doesn't exist.

flex

In a flexbox layout, it's used to display the element like a block-level of a flex container.

5.2 Visibility

Visibility property determines if or not the element is evident without altering the page's layout; moreover, hidden elements consume the space in the website. In <table>, the property may also be used to hide columns or rows. Set a display property with none rather than using visibility to hide and remove an element from the page's layout.

Syntax

It's syntax can be declared by using two properties. These are:

- **Short-hand Property**

visibility: visible|hidden|collapse|initial|inherit;

- **Long-hand Property**

visibility: visible;

visibility: hidden;

visibility: collapse;

visibility: inherit;

Example

Make <h2> elements invisible:

```
h2 {
visibility: hidden;
}
```

Output:

This is a visible heading

Notice that the invisible heading still takes up space.

Values

It's values are as under:

- visible
- hidden
- collapse
- inherit

Brief description of these values are as under:

visible

It's the default value. Visible, as the name implies, makes the contents and it's box visible.

hidden

Even if an element is opaque, it still occupies space. If the element's descendants have visibility adjusted to visible, they will become visible. This is not the same as utilizing display: none, because hidden just hides elements visually. An element is indeed present and occupies space mostly on the website, but it is no longer visible.

collapse

Just table elements can use this property. Collapse eliminates a column or row from the table and has no effect on the layout. The column or row's space would be freed to accommodate other content. The collapse has the same effect as hidden when applied to other elements.

inherit

This is a default value. This essentially means that the element will inherit a value from it's parent, i.e., it will have similar visibility as it's parent.

Chapter 6: Background

It is the most effective and complicated property in CSS. CSS background property allows us to manage the dimensions and attributes of the images, allowing us to make images that are responsive to both smaller and wider screens. As a result, we're able to create more responsive websites. It is also a shorthand property, that means it lets you compose what otherwise would be multiply.

Example

Various background properties can be set in a single declaration such as:

```
body {
    background: #00ff00 url("smiley.gif") no-repeat fixed center;
}
```

Output:

This is some text

This is some text

This is some text

This is some text

This is some text

This is some text

This is some text

This is some text

This is some text

This is some text

This is some text

This is some text

This is some text

This is some text

Syntax

background: value;

Values

Some of it's commonly used values are:

- background-size
- auto-sizing
- background-color
- background-image
- background-position
- background-repeat
- background-attachment

background-size

A background image size is defined here.

Syntax

background-size: cover;

background-size can be used in three different ways:

i. use the Cover/Contain value
ii. set width and height of an image
iii. use auto

This property can be used to adjust the image's width and height.

Syntax

.container{

// here, we see width &   height

  background-size : 200px   200px;

}

auto-sizing

The image would remain at it's initial size while this value is used. When the screen is resized, it won't change anything.

background-color

This property specifies the color of an element's background.

Syntax

.container{

background-color : blue;

}

background-image

One or more background images can be set using this property. Gradients and regular images are the two kinds of images that may be included using CSS.

Syntax

It's simple to use an image as a background like:

```
body {
  background: url(helloworld.jpg);
}
```

The url() attribute enables you to specify the path of a file to some image, which will be used as the element's background.

background-image can be used in two ways:

- By allocating the path of the image inside the directory.
- By giving the URL of an image.

background-position

It's purpose is to adjust the image's location on the window.

Syntax

```
html {
  background-position: 150px 10px;
}
```

Value

There are three kinds of values in it:

- Length values (for example, 100px 5px)
- Percentages (for example, 100% 5%)
- Keywords (for example, top right)

0 0 are it's default values. This positions the background picture in the container's top right corner.

background-repeat

It defines how the background pictures can be repeated.

Syntax

```
html {
```

```
background-image: url(build.png);
background-repeat: repeat-x;
}
```

Value

It consists of six values. Which are as under:

- repeat
- no-repeat
- repeat-x
- repeat-y
- round
- space

background-attachment

It determines whether the document's background is scrolling with it or stays rooted in the display region.

Syntax

```
.container{
background-attachment: scroll;
}
```

This property can be used to adjust the image's height and width.

Value

It consists of three values:

- scroll
- fixed
- local

Chapter 7: Text and Font

CSS's font and text properties control how single characters in a line or word of text appear.

7.1 Text

The text property in CSS is applied to style and format text.

The following properties are used in this property:

- Text-color
- Word spacing
- Letter spacing
- Text-alignment
- Text-decoration
- Line height

7.1.1 Text color

This property is applied to add the text's color.

The name "blue", the hex value "#ff0010" or the RGB value "rgb(190,0,5) can all be used to change the color of the text.

Syntax

body

{

color:color name;

}

Example

h1 {

color: green;

}

7.1.2 Word spacing

The space present in between words of a sentence is described by word spacing. It allows negative values; the value should be in duration format.

Syntax

body

{

word-spacing:size;

}

Examples

P.note { word-spacing: -0.3em }

P EM { word-spacing: 0.6em }

7.1.3 Letter spacing

It is used to determine the amount of space within text characters. Length format must be used for the value. It also allows negative values. A value of 0 disables justification.

Syntax

body

{

letter-spacing:size;

}

Examples

P.note { letter-spacing: -0.1em }

H1 { letter-spacing: 0.1em }

7.1.4 Text-alignment

The use of this property is to adjust the text's horizontal alignment. The text may also be aligned to the right, left, justified or centered.

Syntax

```
body
{
    text-align:alignment type;
    }
```

Example

P.newspaper { text-align: justify }

H1{ text-align: center }

7.1.5 text-decoration

The use of this property is to remove or add decorations from a piece of text. Text may be none, line-through, overline or underlined.

Syntax

```
body
{
text-decoration:decoration type;
}
```

Example

If you don't want to underline the link, then use this;

A:link, A:visited, A:active { text-decoration: none }

7.1.6 line-height

This property sets the line space. Whenever the value is an integer or a number, multiply the font size of the element by it to get a line-height. The percentage value is proportional to the font size of the element. It doesn't allow negative values. Also, with the font size, line height can also be specified with in font property.

Syntax

```
body
{
```

line-height:size;

}

Example

It can be used to add double space to the text. Such as:

P { line-height: 200% }

7.2 Font Property

It is again a shorthand property. Any single value which is not defined is reset to it's initial value, much as any other shorthand property.

Syntax

font: font-style font-weight font-size   font-family|caption|icon|menu|message-box|small-caption|status-bar|initial|inherit;

Example

By using shorthand declaration, you can set certain font properties:

p.a {

font: 15px Arial, sans-serif;

}

p.b {

 font: italic small-caps bold 12px/30px Georgia, serif;

}

Output:

The font Property

This is a paragraph. The font size is set to 15 pixels, and the font family is Arial.

THIS IS A PARAGRAPH. THE FONT IS SET TO ITALIC AND BOLD, WITH SMALL-CAPS (ALL LOWERCASE LETTERS ARE CONVERTED TO UPPERCASE). THE FONT SIZE IS SET TO 12 PIXELS, THE LINE HEIGHT IS SET TO 30 PIXELS, AND THE FONT FAMILY IS GEORGIA.

Values

Some of it's values are:

- font-style
- font-weight
- font-size
- font-family

font-style

This property specifies if a font must be styled by it's italic, oblique or normal face. "Normal" is the default value for this property.

Syntax

It's syntax are as under:

- font-style: normal;
- font-style: italic;
- font-style: oblique;
- font-style: inherit;

font-weight

The thickness or font-weight is defined by this property. "Normal" is the default value of this property. The available weights are determined by the font-family, which is currently identified.

Syntax

Some of it's syntaxes are:

- font-weight: normal;
- font-weight: bold;
- font-weight: lighter;
- font-weight: bolder;

font-size

It specifies the line height and font size are specified. "Natural" is again the default value of this property.

Syntax

Some of it's syntaxes are:

- font-size: small;
- font-size: medium;
- font-size: large;
- font-size: smaller;
- font-size: larger;
- font-size: 12px;
- font-size: 80%;

font-family

It defines the font to be used on the element. It defines a collection of fonts in order of preference, from highest to lowest. The browser determines the default value of the font-family. Since there's no assurance that any particular font would be available, so you have to always add at least a single common family name inside a font-family list. This allows the browser to choose an appropriate fallback font whenever it is required.

Syntax

Some of it's syntaxes are:

- font-family: serif;
- font-family: sans-serif;
- font-family: monospace;
- font-family: cursive;
- font-family: inherit;
- font-family: initial;

Chapter 8: List, links and Navigation bars

Now, let's learn about the list, links and navigation bars.

8.1 Lists

Lists are the common thing in daily life. To-do lists help you figure out what has to be done. Instructions and ingredients are both listed in the recipes. It is indeed easy to see why they're so famous online, with such a list for almost everything. Lists are extremely useful for conveying a series of bullet or numbered points. It enables you to create a list of items for unordered or ordered lists by using separate list object markings. Colors may be added to the background of the lists, and it's list elements. You can also add an image to the list object marker.

8.1.1 List types

There are three types of lists. These are as under:

- **Unordered list**

Unordered lists are used to organize a group of similar items that aren't arranged in any specific order.

- **Ordered list**

Ordered lists are used to organize a group of similar items into a specific order.

- **Description list**

Description lists are used to visualize value or name pairs like definitions and terms.

8.1.2 List style property

Lists can be controlled by using the four Cascading Style Sheets properties that are mentioned below:

- list-style

- list-style-type
- list-style-image
- list-style-position

These are briefly explained below:

- **list-style**

It is the shorthand property. These properties could emerge in any sequence. It sets all of the properties of the list in a single declaration.

Example

ul {

list-style: square inside url("sqpurple.gif");

}

Output:

CSS Lists

The list-style property is a shorthand property, which is used to set all the list properties in one declaration.

- Coffee
- Tea
- Coca Cola

Values

While using a shorthand property, it's values are mentioned in the following order:

list-style-type

list-style-position

list-style-image

If either of the mentioned property values is missing, then it's default value, if any, will be used.

- **list-style-type**

It helps you to manage the marker's appearance or shape. The marker's color is much like the calculated color of an element to which it applies. Furthermore, since as it is an inherited property, it could be applied to every list item by setting it on the parent element.

Example

Set some different list styles:

ul.a {list-style-type: circle;}

ul.b {list-style-type: square;}

ol.c {list-style-type: upper-roman;}

ol.d {list-style-type: lower-alpha;}

Output:

The list-style-type Property

Example of unordered lists:

- Coffee
- Tea
- Coca Cola

- Coffee
- Tea
- Coca Cola

Example of ordered lists:

I. Coffee
II. Tea
III. Coca Cola

a. Coffee
b. Tea
c. Coca Cola

Syntax

list-style-type: value;

Values

A few of them are as under:

disc

- It is a default value

- It is a completely filled circle

circle

- It's an empty circle

square

- It's a completely filled square

decimal

1. These are decimal numbers
2. It begins with 1

lower-roman

i. These are lowercase roman numbers
ii. For example, i, ii, iii, iv, v...

upper-roman

I. These are uppercase roman numbers
II. For example, I, II, III, IV, V...

- **list-style-image**

You may use it to classify an image to apply a customized bullet style. It is not possible to resize the image. It's syntax is identical to that property of the background-image, with the URL preceding the property value and the URL enclosed in brackets. If it is left blank, then none is set by default, which means default bullets are used. Instead of a number or bullet point, it defines an image to set as a marker.

Syntax

list-style-image: value;

Values

It's values are as follow:

none

This property determines that an image can not be used as a list marker. It is used as a default value.

initial

It sets the default value of the property.

url

It is the direction of the image's location, which is used as a marker.

inherit

The value of the element is inherited by their parent element.

Example

Below, we'll go through this property and will look at an example about how to apply it in CSS.

Using List Items

You may also apply this property to a list item directly, as given here:

li { list-style-image: url("/images/symbol.gif"); }

This will also lead to the following list items emerging (irrespective of if a list item is ordered (sorted) or unordered):

- TechOnTheNet.com
- CheckYourMath.com
- BigActivities.com

In this example, the circle from the rear of every list item in a <ul> tag would be exchanged with the blue.gif image.

- **list-style-position**

This property specifies if the marker must be placed within or outside the bullet-point box. It determines if a large point which wraps to the second line can coincide with it's first line or begin underneath the marker's start.

Syntax

It's syntax is as under:

Values

It consists of three values. These are as under:

- Outside
- inside
- inherit

outside

Marker box should be on the outside of the main block box. It is set by default.

Syntax

ul { list-style-position: outside; }

inside

Marker box should be located within the main block box.

Syntax

ul { list-style-position: inside; }

inherit

List-style-position of an element is inherited from it's own parent element.

Syntax:

ol { list-style-position: inherit; }

8.2 Links

A link is an attachment between two or more web pages. CSS properties may be applied to style attachments in a variety of ways. Buttons or boxes may also be applied to style CSS links.

8.2.1 The Link's States

Links could exist in various states

The following are the four states of the links:

a:link

It is a regular link that hasn't been visited.

Syntax

```
a:link {
    color:color_name;
}
```

a:hover

It's a link when the mouse floats over it.

Syntax

```
a:hover {
    color:color_name;
}
```

a:visited

It is the link that a user has visited at-least once.

Syntax

```
a:visited {
    color:color_name;
}
```

a:active

It is a recently clicked link.

Syntax

a:active {

    color:color_name;

}

Links defaults values:

- All links created by default are underlined.
- The hand icon appears when the mouse is floated over a link.
- Links that haven't been accessed are blue in color.
- Purple colored links are those who have been visited.
- Active links are represented by red color.
- A focused link is surrounded by an outline.

8.2.2 Links Properties

The following are some basic CSS properties for the links:

- text-decoration
- color
- background-color
- font-family

text-decoration

The purpose of this property is to remove or add underlines from the link.

Syntax

```
a {
    text-decoration: none;
}
```

color

The color of the link text can be changed by using it.

Syntax

```
a {
    color: color_name;
}
```

background-color

It sets the color of the link's background.

Syntax

```
a {
    background-color: color_name;
}
```

font-family

Using this property, you may modify a font type of the link.

Syntax:

```
a {
    font-family: "family name";
}
```

8.3 Navigation Bar

As a foundation, a navigation bar requires standard HTML. A collection of links which lead to various pages of the website is referred to as a navigation bar in CSS. Horizontal or vertical navigation bars are available.

By two elements, HTML forms the framework of a navigation bar. These are as under:

- <ul>
- <li>

Example 1

```
<ul>
  <li><a href="default.asp">Home</a></li>
  <li><a href="news.asp">News</a></li>
  <li><a href="contact.asp">Contact</a></li>
  <li><a href="about.asp">About</a></li>
</ul>
```

Output:

- Home
- News
- Contact
- About

Note: We use href="#" for test links. In a real web site this would be URLs.

Now exclude the bullets, as well as the padding and margins from a list:

Example 2

ul {

list-style-type: none;

margin: 0;

padding: 0;

}

Output:

In this example, we remove the bullets from the list, and its default padding and margin.

Home
News
Contact
About

It's essential to disable the default navigation bar settings of the browser.

Example explained

list-style-type:

Bullets are removed when none value is applied to the navigation bars.

margin: 0; and padding: 0;

It removes the existing or default spacing settings of the browser

Both horizontal and vertical navigation bars have these properties. The coding in the previous example is common for both horizontal and vertical navigation bars.

Chapter 9: Tables

In HTML, a <table> is used to view tabular data. It's a means of describing and displaying data that can be useful in spreadsheet applications. Or a nutshell, there are rows and columns.

Example

Below is a quick example of the tabular data:

```
<table>
  <tr>
    <th>Name</th>
    <th>ID</th>
    <th>Favorite Color</th>
  </tr>
  <tr>
    <td>Jim</td>
    <td>00001</td>
    <td>Blue</td>
  </tr>
  <tr>
    <td>Sue</td>
    <td>00002</td>
    <td>Red</td>
  </tr>
  <tr>
    <td>Barb</td>
    <td>00003</td>
    <td>Green</td>
  </tr>
```

```
</table>
```

Output:

Name	ID	Favorite Color
Jim	00001	Blue
Sue	00002	Red
Barb	00003	Green

9.1 Table Borders

Border property of CSS is used to define table borders.

For the <table>, <td>, and <th> components, the following example defines the black border:

Example

```
table, th, td {
  border: 1px solid black;
}
```

Output:

Add a border to a table:

Firstname	Lastname
Peter	Griffin
Lois	Griffin

9.2 Table Padding

Use this property upon on <td> and th> elements to manage the space within the content and the border in the table.

Example

th, td {

 padding: 15px;

 text-align: left;

}

Output:

The padding Property

This property adds space between the border and the content in a table.

Firstname	Lastname	Savings
Peter	Griffin	$100
Lois	Griffin	$150
Joe	Swanson	$300
Cleveland	Brown	$250

9.3 Table Alignment

There are two types of table alignments. These are:

- Horizontal alignment
- Vertical alignment

Now let's discuss them in detail:

9.3.1 Horizontal Alignment

This property specifies a horizontal alignment of the material in <td> or <th> (such as right, left, or centre). The composition of the <th> elements is center-aligned by default, while the composition of <td> elements is left-aligned. Using text-align: center; to align the material or content of the <td> component(element).

Example 1

```
td {
text-align: center;
}
```

Output:

The text-align Property

This property sets the horizontal alignment (like left, right, or center) of the content in th or td.

Firstname	Lastname	Savings
Peter	Griffin	$100
Lois	Griffin	$150
Joe	Swanson	$300
Cleveland	Brown	$250

For left-aligning a content, use text-align: left property; to push the alignment of the <th> elements so that it can be left-aligned.

Example 2

```
th {
text-align: left;
}
```

Output:

The text-align Property

This property sets the horizontal alignment (like left, right, or center) of the content in th or td.

Firstname	Lastname	Savings
Peter	Griffin	$100
Lois	Griffin	$150
Joe	Swanson	$300
Cleveland	Brown	$250

9.3.2 Vertical Alignment

Vertical-align property determines how the content in <td> or <th> is aligned vertically (such as bottom, middle or top). Vertical alignment is set to middle by default (for both <td> and <th> elements) of content that is present in the table.

Example:

td {

height: 50px;

vertical-align: bottom;

}

Output:

The vertical-align Property

This property sets the vertical alignment (like top, bottom, or middle) of the content in th or td.

Firstname	Lastname	Savings
Peter	Griffin	$100
Lois	Griffin	$150
Joe	Swanson	$300
Cleveland	Brown	$250

9.4 Table Width and Height

The height and width properties describe the height and height of the table.

Width of a table is set to 100%, as well as height of <th> elements is set to 70px in the example given below:

Example 1

```
table {
  width: 100%;
}


th {
  height: 70px;
}
```

Output:

The width and height Properties

Set the width of the table, and the height of the table header row:

Firstname	Lastname	Savings
Peter	Griffin	$100
Lois	Griffin	$150
Joe	Swanson	$300
Cleveland	Brown	$250

Using width: 50%, to make a table which just covers half of the page in the following example.

Example 2

```
table {
  width: 50%;
}
```

```
th {
  height: 70px;
}
```

Output:

The width and height Properties

Set the width of the table, and the height of the table header row:

Firstname	Lastname	Savings
Peter	Griffin	$100
Lois	Griffin	$150
Joe	Swanson	$300
Cleveland	Brown	$250

Conclusion

HyperText Markup Language and Cascading Style Sheets are both used to create a website or web page. CSS, on the other hand, is trying to replace HTML because it has more flexibility and features. Consider CSS to be the color of the paint, window designs, and landscaping that falls after the base, doors, partitions, and girders that protect the website. You won't get far without laying the foundation, but when you do, then you would like to add some design. Cascading Style Sheets are the key to bringing out your inner designer. Who'd have guessed that HTML and CSS are such large subjects? If you came this far, you're on your road to mastering the front end production of a website. You can be even more at ease analysing and breaking the structure of the website into it's individual components and thereafter coding them in CSS. You now have the tools you need to define and implement an effective visual interface. You do have a lot of room to develop your skills and your understanding of best practices, so don't quit practicing and learning, yet you have all you need to create stunning websites with the help of Cascading Style Sheets.

In conclusion, all we can say is that the Cascading Style Sheets helps you customize your web page or website. It makes your web page look presentable to the users, and it also attracts new users by it's look and feel. It makes your web page look different from other web pages and makes it user friendly. It is easier than other languages because it lessens the amount of coding to enhance it's website's look because a single line of code can be used to change the whole or part of the website at once when required. It also has some shorthand properties, which are really helpful to shorten the code, and it saves a lot of web designers time and effort. As it helps to style text, fonts and coloring of a website, it also helps us to position, float, set backgrounds, style different types of lists, navigation bars and tables.

www.ingramcontent.com/pod-product-compliance
Lightning Source LLC
LaVergne TN
LVHW082035050326
832904LV00005B/188